THE ULTIMATE KID'S GUIDE TO THE UNIVERSE

BY JENNY MARDER

GROSSET & DUNLAP

GROSSET & DUNLAP
An imprint of Penguin Random House LLC, New York

First published in the United States of America by Grosset & Dunlap,
an imprint of Penguin Random House LLC, New York, 2024

Text copyright © 2024 by Jennifer Marder

Cover photo credits: front cover (clockwise from top right corner): (Tarantula Nebula)
NASA/ESA/CSA/STScI/Webb ERO Production Team, (NGC 7250 and Lizard Star)
ESA/Hubble/NASA, (Southern Ring Nebula) NASA/ESA/CSA/STScI, (Cosmic Cliffs)
NASA/ESA/CSA/STScI, (Apollo 8: Earthrise) NASA, (ESA astronaut Matthias Maurer)
NASA Johnson/Flickr; back cover: (Proxima Centauri) ESA/Hubble/NASA

Interior icon credits: used throughout: (heads icon) appleuzr/DigitalVision
Vectors/Getty Images, (space icons) studiostockart/DigitalVision Vectors/Getty Images,
Turac Novruzova/iStock/Getty Images; 9: (top) Peacefully7/iStock/Getty Images,
(bottom) RLT_Images/DigitalVision Vectors/Getty Images

GROSSET & DUNLAP is a registered trademark of Penguin Random House LLC.

Visit us online at penguinrandomhouse.com.

Library of Congress Cataloging-in-Publication Data is available.

Manufactured in China

ISBN 9780593658925   10 9 8 7 6 5 4 3 2 1 TOPL

Design by Taylor Abatiell and Abby Dening

CONTENTS

WHEN DAY BECOMES NIGHT

Every now and then, if you're in the exact right place at the exact right time, something extraordinary happens. It's the middle of the day, but the light outside turns silver gray and then gets darker, as if a giant umbrella is moving over the sky.

The wind stops. The temperature drops. It gets eerily quiet. Chickens return to their coops, horses and cows to their barns. Bats appear in the sky. Crickets chirp. Dogs howl. Squirrels run in circles, confused. In the ocean, dolphins swim to the surface and look up.

Your shadow gets long and curved and weird. Meanwhile, you might see ripples of shimmering light, called shadow bands, moving across the ground or the mountains.

A total solar eclipse

NASA/Aubrey Gemignani

A boy watches a solar eclipse.

Outside, the sky gets even darker. For several minutes, it's as dark as a moonlit night. The sun, the force that gives us life, is gone, as if time has stopped.

In the sky, where the sun used to be, is a tiny, black circle. Around that circle are shimmery threads, like tentacles of light. And then it's over, and everything goes back to normal.

This is a **total solar eclipse**.

A total solar eclipse occurs when the moon moves between the Earth and the sun and, for a few minutes, the three are perfectly lined up. During this time, the moon blocks the sun's light entirely.

The wispy threads around the sun are the **corona**. The corona is the sun's outer atmosphere, and a total solar eclipse is also the only time we can see the corona with our own eyes. The corona is unimaginably hot, more than two million degrees Fahrenheit. That's even hotter than the surface of the sun, which is about ten thousand degrees Fahrenheit. From the corona comes solar wind, which streams into space.

Thousands of years ago, people found solar eclipses terrifying and magical. In ancient China, it was thought that a dragon had swallowed the sun. Ancient Greeks thought the king was being punished. But solar eclipses also inspired early scientists to search for patterns and clues in the night sky.

DiD YOU KNOW?

A solar eclipse happens because of a strange and lucky coincidence. The moon is four hundred times smaller than the sun, but it's also about four hundred times closer to Earth. The result is that during a solar eclipse, they look like they're the same size in the sky.

From these patterns came **astronomy**, the study of stars and planets and space.

In this book, we'll take you on a tour of the night sky. We'll learn about the universe we live in, the unimaginable bigness of it, and how we fit in. We'll learn about the planets in our solar system and their moons. We'll learn about the brave humans who have traveled to space. We'll explore whether aliens might exist. And we'll learn about the search for worlds beyond our own planet Earth.

CHAPTER ONE

THE NIGHT SKY

I f you've seen the movie *The Lion King*, you might remember the part when Simba the lion and his friends are relaxing in the tall grass, looking up at the stars in the night sky.

"Ever wonder what those sparkly dots are up there?" Pumbaa the warthog asks. "They're fireflies, fireflies that got stuck," Timon the meerkat replies. "Oh, gee," Pumbaa says, "I always thought they were balls of gas burning billions of miles away."

Pumbaa got it right. A **star** is a big, glowing ball of hot gas. Each star is a distant sun, like our own. In the night sky, stars look like tiny pinpricks of light because they're incredibly far away from us.

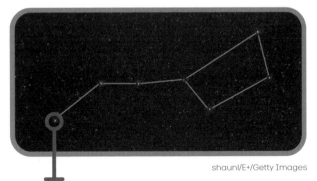

shaunl/E+/Getty Images

You can see **Polaris**, the North Star, in the constellation Ursa Minor, also known as the Little Dipper.

It's fun to explore the night sky with binoculars or a telescope, but there's also so much you can see with just your eyes. You can see stars, the moon, and even a shooting star (if you're lucky!). You can see **constellations**—groups of stars that form pictures. Also, depending on the time, you can see five of the planets in our solar system: Mercury, Venus, Mars, Jupiter, and Saturn.

In this chapter, we're going to give you the tools to wow your friends and stump your family with your stargazing skills.

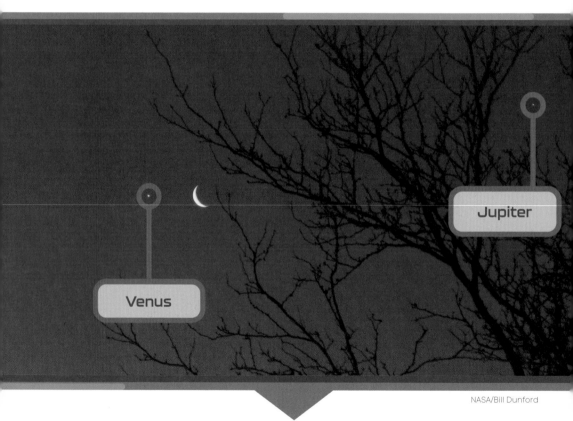

NASA/Bill Dunford

Look to see Venus on the left, a crescent moon in the middle, and Jupiter on the right side of the sky above Salt Lake City, Utah.

Stargazing: A Quick How-To

You need to pick the right spot and the right night. Choose a night when the sky is clear of clouds. Little to no moonlight is best. If you can, find a place away from buildings and tall trees, streetlights and car headlights. Try a large backyard, a rooftop, or an open field. The more sky you can see, the better. If you're outside your home, turn off all the lights—and check with your grown-ups to see if it's okay to ask your neighbors to turn off theirs, too.

STARGAZING TOOL KIT

- ■ Insect repellent
- ■ A blanket, towel, or folding chair
- ■ Warm socks, sweater, jacket, and hat (depending on time of year)
- ■ **Red-light flashlight**: A flashlight with a red lens helps you see your way and read a star chart without losing your night vision. (See page 13 to make a homemade red-light flashlight.)
- ■ Water and snacks

Now get comfortable and look up. Give your eyes some time to adjust to the dark. What do you see? If you're in a city, you might only see a handful of bright stars. That's because city lights make

The night sky above **Lake Tekapo**, New Zealand. Lake Tekapo is known for its clear night skies, perfect for stargazing.

the sky brighter, blocking out starlight. That's called **light pollution**. Away from city lights, you can probably see thousands of stars. Either way, the longer you look, the more stars you'll see.

When a major earthquake struck Los Angeles before sunrise in 1994, most of the city lost power. Without city lights, people walked outside to find the sky full of stars. Emergency call centers were flooded with callers asking about a strange, glowing cloud. Don't worry, they were told. It was just the Milky Way. They were seeing a band of light from our galaxy.

Consider these two questions as you look up.

1. ARE ALL THE STARS YOU SEE EQUALLY BRIGHT?

No, they're not. Some stars appear bigger and brighter in our sky than others. This is because of two things: their distance from us and how much energy they put out, or their **luminosity**.

DISTANCE: Think of two identical cars driving toward you at night. If one of the cars is closer, its headlights will look bigger and brighter than the other, even though they're the same size. Their distance from you changes the way they appear.

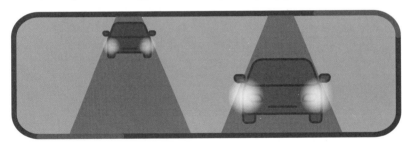

LUMINOSITY: Now imagine a car headlight and a flashlight, both placed ten feet away. The headlight appears bigger because it *is* bigger and brighter. It's emitting more energy. In this case, its luminosity is what makes it appear bigger.

Some stars might appear brighter because they're closer to us. That's true for **Alpha Centauri** (say: **sen-TOUR-ee**), the closest star system to our sun. But more often, they appear brighter because they're bigger than other stars and are giving off more light. **Betelgeuse**, for example, (say: **BEE-tel-juice**) is a star that's 160 times farther away from us than Alpha Centauri, but it's massive—887 times larger than our sun. It is one of the most luminous stars in our sky.

Sirius, the brightest star in our sky is bright because it's both close and luminous.

Sound Smart

Alpha Centauri looks like one star, but it is actually a star system made up of three stars that are close together: Alpha Centauri A (left), Alpha Centauri B (right), and Proxima Centauri (not shown).

ESA/NASA

DiD YOU KNOW?

Most of the brightest stars are not nearby, and many of the closest stars aren't all that bright.

2. ARE ALL STARS THE SAME COLOR?

They're all white, right? Wrong! Look again. Some appear slightly blue. Some appear slightly red. Some are more orange. This is because they have different temperatures. Hotter stars look blue or white. Cooler stars look orange or red. The temperatures also tell us about where a star is in its life cycle.

A bright star outshines a distant galaxy named NGC 7250.

ESA/Hubble/NASA

The James Webb Space Telescope's Near-Infrared Camera (NIRCam) captured this image of the Tarantula Nebula star-forming region.

NASA/ESA/CSA/STScI/Webb ERO Production Team

Different Types of Stars

NEBULA: Stars are born in clouds of gas and dust. These nurseries where stars are born are called **stellar nebulas**. Nebulas occur during star death, too. A **planetary nebula** comes from gas and dust shed from the outer layers of a dying star.

YELLOW DWARF: Our sun is a type of star called a yellow dwarf.

RED DWARF: Red dwarfs are the smallest type of stars and they make up most of the stars in our galaxy.

RED GIANT: When our sun begins to run out of fuel, it will temporarily become a red giant, a large red star. Most stars become red giants before collapsing as white dwarfs or exploding as supernovas.

WHITE DWARF: A white dwarf is the slowly cooling core of a small or medium star that has recently died. At the end of its life, many billions of years from now, our sun will gently shed its outer layers to space, leaving behind the white dwarf at its center.

SUPERNOVA: The largest supergiant stars explode powerfully into supernovas at the end of their lives, violently flinging their outer layers to space in explosions that can briefly outshine entire galaxies.

NEUTRON STAR: The hot, very dense core left behind after massive stars explode in supernovas.

BLACK HOLE: When the most massive stars run out of fuel, they collapse into black holes after exploding in supernovas. A black hole is an extremely dense object with a gravitational pull so strong that nothing, not even light, can escape it.

ESA/Hubble/NASA

This Hubble Space Telescope image shows our closest stellar neighbor, Proxima Centauri.

Try This at Home: Throw a Star Party.

- Find a place away from lights with big, open sky.
- If you know anyone with a telescope, invite them!
- Bring popcorn, a thermos of hot chocolate, and cookies shaped like stars and moons.
- Bring flashlights, rubber bands, and red cellophane for a red-light flashlight activity. You can make your own red-light flashlight by wrapping red cellophane around the light of a regular flashlight with rubber bands. Do this activity as the sun sets, and don't turn on the flashlight until the red cellophane is covering the light. Your eyes are adjusting and getting their night vision.
- Lay out blankets and set up folding chairs.

THAT'S IT! THE SKY WILL DO THE REST.

Is It a Star or a Planet?

The brightest star you see might not be a star at all. It might be a planet, such as Mars or Venus. Planets look like extra bright stars. This is because you're seeing the sun reflected off them. So how can you tell the difference?

Look closely. Is it a steady light or is it twinkling? A planet doesn't twinkle like a star. Planets are closer than stars, so they appear larger and their light steadier. Also, stars stay in the same spots in relation to other stars. Planets seem to wander around the sky as they orbit our sun, constantly changing their positions.

This illustration shows a Jupiter-Venus conjuction as it appears looking east in Huntsville, Alabama, on the morning of April 30, 2022. You can see how the planets follow a line.

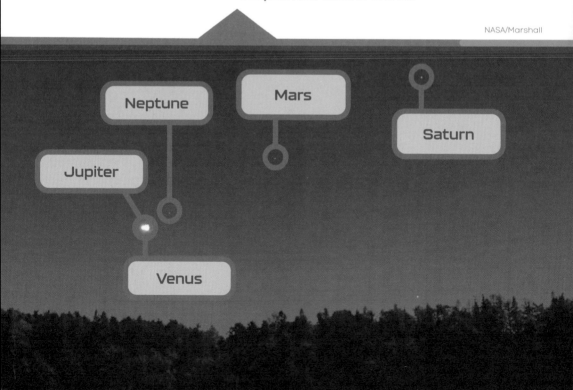

But if you watch the planets closely over time, you'll see that they move across the sky in a line. That's because the planets go around our sun in a nice, neat orbit. An **orbit** is the path an object takes as it goes around another object. So if you figure out where in the sky to look, that's where the planets will always be. This line that they move across is called the **ecliptic**.

To find the ecliptic, look for where the sun rises and sets. The planets will move across the same line as the sun, but more slowly.

If you can get your hands on a telescope, or even good-quality binoculars, you can actually see Saturn's rings, Jupiter's red spot, and sometimes even Jupiter's moons.

NASA/JPL/Southwest
Research Institute

A view of **Saturn** taken by NASA's Cassini spacecraft

Star Distance

Stars are really, *really* far away, and you need the right unit of distance to measure just how far. If you wanted to measure the length of a sneaker or a Pokémon card, you'd take out a ruler and measure in centimeters or inches, right? But now, imagine you wanted to measure the distance from your house to your school. Inches don't cut it anymore. You need a larger unit of distance—like miles.

To measure the distance between objects in our own solar system, we use what's called an **astronomical unit**. One astronomical unit, or AU, is the average distance between the Earth and the sun. That's ninety-three million miles.

LIGHT-YEARS

■ But stars are so far away that measuring them in miles or even astronomical units won't get us anywhere near far enough. So we use **light-years**. A light-year sounds like a unit of time, but it's actually a way of measuring distance. One light-year is the distance that light travels in one year. And light moves fast—about 186,000 miles every second—so that's a really long distance.

THINK OF IT THIS WAY: It takes about eight minutes for light to travel from the sun to the Earth. So the sun is eight light-minutes away. It takes about a second for the light from the moon to reach us on Earth, so the moon is one light-second away.

Compared to a light-second or light-minute, a light-*year* is a truly enormous unit of distance. One light-year is nearly six *trillion* miles. Proxima Centauri, the closest star to our sun, is about four light-years away. That means something traveling the speed of light would take four years to travel from Earth to that star. For now, we know of nothing that can travel faster than the speed of light.

Time Traveling

Remember that it takes eight minutes for light from the sun to reach Earth. That means when we're looking at the sun, we're seeing it as it was eight minutes ago. If we're seeing a star that's four light-years away, we're seeing the star as it looked four years ago. And if we're looking at a star that's tens, hundreds, or thousands of light-years away—as many of them are—we're seeing them tens or hundreds or thousands of years ago. That's how long it took for their light to travel the vast distance of space to reach us.

It's fascinating, isn't it? When we look into space, we're looking *back in time*. We're time traveling.

In fact, with some of the faraway stars we see through telescopes, we're looking so far back in time that what we're looking at *no longer exists*.

ALPHA CENTAURI: 4.4 light-years away

SIRIUS: 8.6 light-years away

POLARIS, NORTH STAR: 323 light-years away

BETELGEUSE: 724 light-years away

NOTE: GRAPHIC IS NOT TO SCALE

Constellations

When stargazing, it's also fun to look for constellations, or groups of stars that appear to be clustered in a recognizable pattern. Constellations are named after all sorts of things: animals and Greek gods and kitchen utensils. And if you were to draw a line from star to star—and really use your imagination—you'd see how the stars form shapes.

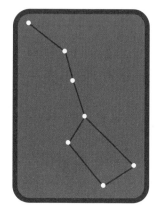

Sound Smart

The Andromeda galaxy, the nearest major galaxy to ours, is 2.5 million light-years away. So we're seeing it as it was 2.5 million years ago.

NASA/JPL-Caltech

The Andromeda galaxy, or M31

We're about to show you how to search for some of the most common constellations.

But before we do, let's set the record straight. The constellations we see are only visible from our solar system. And the stars that make up a constellation have no actual relation to one another. In fact, two stars sitting right next to each other in a constellation could easily be farther apart than two stars at opposite ends of our sky. For this reason, many astronomers don't much care about them.

Still, constellations are fun, and they help you find your way around the sky. Here are some star patterns and clues for how to spot them.

THE BiG DiPPER

The Big Dipper is part of the constellation Ursa Major, and it is one of the easiest patterns to spot in the sky on a clear night. The star pattern creates a large bowl and handle. And the two stars that make up the bottom of the dipper are called the Pointers because they point directly to **Polaris**, the North Star.

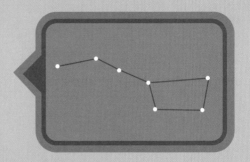

POLaRiS

Draw a line between the Pointer stars, and then follow it about five times as far, and you'll reach Polaris. Polaris is known as the North Star because Earth's North Pole always points toward it. Polaris, like Alpha Centauri, looks like one star, but it's really part of a star system of three stars: Polaris Aa, Polaris Ab, and Polaris B.

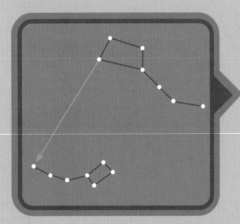

LittLe DiPPER

Polaris makes up the very tip of the Little Dipper, or Ursa Minor. Like the Big Dipper, the Little Dipper is made up of seven stars that form a handle and bowl, but it is smaller and not as bright.

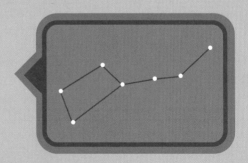

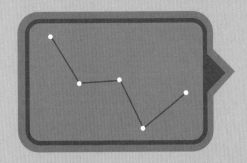

OriON

Orion looks like a hunter, holding a sword, shield, and bow. Face south and look for three equally spaced bright stars. That's Orion's belt. The two bright stars above his belt are his shoulders, and the two bright stars below are his feet. Betelgeuse is its eastern shoulder. Rigel is its opposite foot. Betelgeuse looks reddish, and Rigel looks bluish compared to typical stars that look more white.

CASSIOPEIA (THE QUEEN)

Find the Pointer stars at the end of the Big Dipper again. Trace a line to Polaris. Continue past Polaris about the same distance. The group of five stars forming a stretched-out *W* or *M* shape is Cassiopeia.

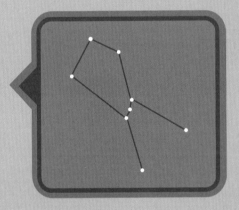

THE TWINS

Gemini, also known as the Twins, looks like two people holding hands. Their heads are made up of the stars Castor and Pollux. And a line drawn from Betelgeuse and Rigel points to these bright heads.

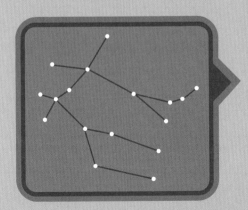

Some Other Things You Can See in the Night Sky

Satellite

Satellites move quickly across the sky. (But if the light is blinking, it's probably an airplane.)

Comet

A comet is like a giant, dirty snowball whose ice is evaporating. Comets, like planets, move so slowly across our sky that you can't see them moving.

NASA/Bill Dunford

Comet NEOWISE seen on July 9, 2020, over Deer Valley, Utah

Asteroid

An asteroid is a small, rocky object that orbits the sun like a planet. Most can be found in the asteroid belt between Mars and Jupiter. You can sometimes see the giant asteroid Vesta with your own eyes. Others require binoculars or a small telescope.

Shooting Star

"Shooting stars" are chunks from comets and asteroids, and they can be seen any time of year if you're lucky. They're not actually stars, but rather meteors in Earth's atmosphere. Shooting stars zip by so fast that you can easily miss them.

Meteor Shower

When Earth crosses a comet's orbit, there's lots of dust and debris. That's when you can catch a meteor shower.

Milky Way

You can see part of our Milky Way galaxy on a clear night if you're in a place with little light pollution. It looks like a curved cloud or a silver river stretching across the sky.

A shooting star (meteor) zooms by during the Perseid meteor shower on August 11, 2021.

NASA/Bill Ingalls

The **Milky Way** visible in the sky in Canyonlands National Park

NPS/Kait Thomas

CHAPTER TWO

"WE ARE STAR STUFF"

Look around you. Nearly everything you see was cooked inside the bellies of distant stars. Iron is in that metal doorknob; hydrogen is in the pages of this book. And that last cookie you ate? It had carbon in it, which basically means you were eating star guts.

Let's back up. A long time ago, 13.8 billion years ago, all the energy of the universe was packed into a hot, dense point, smaller than the tip of a pencil. Suddenly it began to grow, fast, like taffy being stretched, but in every direction. For a split second, the universe expanded faster than the speed of light, and then kept expanding.

DiD YOU KNOW?

A billion is a *very* large number. It is a one followed by nine zeros. So 13.8 billion looks like this: 13,800,000,000.

24

DiD YOU KNOW?

A single atom is so tiny that even the most powerful microscope can't see it.

It was the beginning of the universe as we know it. This event is known as the **big bang**.

For one hundred million years after the big bang, the universe was a cold, lonely place. All that existed were clouds of dust made of hydrogen and helium gas (and a tiny bit of a gas called lithium). It was pitch-black because there were no stars yet. It smelled like nothing. But it kept growing. And as time went on, things started to take shape.

Sound Smart

To understand the biggest stuff in the universe, you need to know about the smallest. Everything you see is made up of **atoms**. Atoms themselves are made of three main parts: protons, neutrons, and electrons. The first atoms were created not long after the big bang.

There are lots of different kinds of atoms, but these very first atoms, hydrogen and helium, were the simplest. Hydrogen has just one proton and one electron. Helium has two protons, two neutrons, and two electrons. Over time, bigger, heavier atoms were created inside stars. Iron, for example, has twenty-six protons, thirty neutrons, and twenty-six electrons.

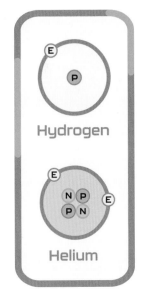

Hydrogen

Helium

Gravity

You can't understand anything happening in space without understanding **gravity**. On Earth, gravity is what keeps us on the ground and makes things fall. In space, it pulls objects together, sort of like a magnet. The more massive an object, the stronger its pull. The same force that allows you to dribble a basketball is what keeps the moon in orbit around the Earth and holds entire galaxies together.

Remember those clouds of dust in the ancient universe? Over time, gravity caused some of the clouds to collapse in on themselves.

And then something incredible happened. They started to shine from within. These were the very first stars.

Stars make heat and light through a process called nuclear fusion in which small atoms smash together to make larger ones. Hydrogen atoms smash together, forming helium and releasing huge amounts of heat in the process, which creates pressure. That pressure pushes the star outward while gravity pushes it inward, holding the star together.

That's What We Know.
Here's What We Don't Know:

We don't know what happened before the big bang. We also don't know for sure what caused the big bang. All we know is that something changed 13.8 billion years ago, and the universe began to expand.

This image by NASA's James Webb Space Telescope, known as Cosmic Cliffs, shows a stellar nursery, an area of star birth, where young stars are forming.

NASA/ESA/CSA/STScI

NASA/ESA/CSA/STScI

A star, remember, is a big, glowing ball of hot gas. The earliest stars were giant, much bigger than our sun. They were made of mostly hydrogen and helium, the simplest atoms and the ones that were created in the big bang. And when these ancient stars burned off all their hydrogen, they started to die.

There are two main ways that stars die.

Smaller stars gently puff off their outer layers while their inner core collapses. All that's left of these stars is their once-hot core. These are white dwarfs.

Other larger stars blow themselves apart and blast their materials out into space. These spectacular star deaths are called supernovas.

As more stars were born and died, they created new, more complex atoms, like iron, carbon, and oxygen, and scattered them across space.

NASA's Hubble Space Telescope captured this white dwarf star called Sirius B.

NASA/ESA/H. Bond (STScI)/M. Barstow (University of Leicester)

These are the atoms that make up the iron in our blood, the carbon in our bones, and the oxygen we breathe.

That's what the famous astronomer Carl Sagan meant when he said, "We are made of star stuff." Atoms that were cooked inside stars are now inside of us. And they are the building blocks of everything we can see in the universe.

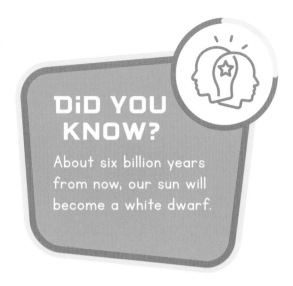

The Universe

The universe is bigger than you can possibly imagine. But let's try.

Think about planet Earth. Our enormous planet that contains oceans and mountains and elephants and soccer fields and snow cones and 7.7 billion people.

NASA

The South Polar ice cap, the Arabian Peninsula, and nearly the entire coastline of Africa can be seen in this image of Earth, captured by the crew of Apollo 17 on Dec. 7, 1972.

Now imagine 109 of these Earths lined up side by side. That's how many Earths would fit across the face of the sun.

Just like people live in neighborhoods, our sun and Earth are part of a **solar system**. Our solar system is made up of the sun and eight planets, along with lots of asteroids, comets, and dwarf planets. And just like each neighborhood is part of a bigger city, each solar system is part of a bigger **galaxy**. Our solar system is located in a Frisbee-shaped galaxy called the Milky Way.

NASA/Adler/U. Chicago/Wesleyan/ JPL-Caltech

This graphic shows our Milky Way galaxy. The sun is located in a part of the galaxy called the "Orion Spur."

Galaxies

The only way to even picture the size of our galaxy is to imagine that the sun is the size of the period at the end of this sentence and everything else is shrunk down to that scale. On this tiny scale, the closest star, Proxima Centauri, would still be ten miles away. And the distance across the Milky Way galaxy would stretch from the Earth to the moon.

These stars are just two of more than a hundred *billion* stars in our Milky Way galaxy. Yikes.

NASA/ESA/CSA/STScI

You can see thousands of galaxies in this image taken by the James Webb Space Telescope.

And if that makes you feel small, consider this: Our galaxy is one of millions and millions of galaxies in the universe.

Take a look at this image above captured by NASA's James Webb Space Telescope.

Webb stared at a tiny pinprick of the sky and beamed this back. Each of these dots is not a star, but a galaxy. Just this tiny part of the sky shows thousands of galaxies.

DiD YOU KNOW?

Did you know that galaxies eat other galaxies? Ten billion years ago, our Milky Way galaxy ate another galaxy, called Gaia-Enceladus. And in about four billion years, our neighboring galaxy, Andromeda, will eat us, the Milky Way.

This artist's rendition shows our galaxy, the Milky Way, colliding with the neighboring Andromeda galaxy.

NASA/ESA/A. Feild/R. van der Marel/STScI

The Universe Is Expanding

Remember how the universe started its life by growing? Well, it hasn't stopped. A hundred years ago, astronomers discovered that nearly all galaxies were rushing away from us at high speeds. More recently, astronomers learned that this expansion is getting faster. Everything in the universe is rushing away from everything else.

Try This at Home:
The Reverse Big Bang Balloon Experiment

Draw a bunch of dots on a balloon. Each dot represents a galaxy. Then blow up the balloon. See how all the dots move away from each other? That's how the universe is expanding. Now, let go of the balloon, and watch it shrink. Watch the galaxies get close together again. What you're seeing now is the big bang in reverse.

This doesn't mean that our bodies are stretching. And it doesn't mean that Earth or our solar system or even our galaxy itself is expanding. Think of a Froot Loops necklace on an elastic string. If you pull both sides of the string, the Froot Loops move apart from each other. But the Froot Loops themselves don't stretch. Like our cereal example, our planets and solar systems and galaxies are held together by gravity, so they're not expanding. It's the space between the galaxies that's flying apart.

A duck swims across a lake at sunset.

Planets

Back to the early universe. Billions of years ago, from a swirling disk of gas and ancient stardust, our sun was born. Over time, leftover clumps of gas and dust swirling around the sun crashed into each other and stuck together, making planets and moons. Some clumps made the outer planets, such as Saturn and Neptune and Jupiter.

But closer to the sun was a special planet. It was just far enough from the sun that it wasn't too hot or too cold, and—and this is important—it could support liquid water. All living things need water to survive, and this planet had a lot of it.

In time, molten rock from volcanoes cooled and became islands, warm water oceans formed, plants sprouted from the soil. Bugs appeared, and animals and, eventually, people.

It was our planet Earth, and it was beautiful.

CHapTER THREE

OUR PLACE IN THE UNIVERSE

Nearly every picture and poster and puzzle you've seen of our solar system is wrong. They're distorted. In these pictures, planets look close together and similar in size. But the true scale of our solar system boggles the mind.

CONSIDER THIS: If Earth were the size of a baseball, the moon would be the size of a marble and the sun would fill a three-story house. At this scale, the moon would be seven feet away from Earth, about the height of a front door. And the sun would be half a mile, or seven soccer fields, away. Meanwhile, Neptune, the farthest known planet in our solar system, would be seventeen miles away.

Let's back up. Our sun is 4.6 billion years old and located ninety-three million miles from Earth. It is the largest object in our solar system, so big that more than a million Earths could fit inside it.

Its gravity holds together our entire solar system. Revolving around the sun are eight planets, five dwarf planets, tens of thousands of asteroids, and a trillion comets.

In this chapter, we'll take you on a tour of our solar system, the part of space we know best.

Our Solar System

Amy Moran/NASA/Johns Hopkins University Applied Physics Laboratory/Carnegie Institution of Washington (Mercury), USGS Astrogeology Science Center (Venus, Mars), NASA's Goddard Space Flight Center/Space Telescope Science Institute (Jupiter), NASA/JPL/Space Science Institute (Saturn), NASA's Goddard Space Flight Center (Earth, Jupiter, Uranus)

Mercury
Messenger
2011

Venus
Magellan
1990–1992

Earth
S-NPP VIIRS
2015

Mars
Viking/Mars Mosaiced
Digital Image Model
(MDIM)
1975/2014

Jupiter
Hubble Space
Telescope
2015

Saturn
Cassini-Huygen
2000 (planet)
2007 (rings)

Uranus
W.M. Keck Observatory
2004

Neptune
Voyager
1989

Pluto
New Horizons
2015

Solar means anything related to the sun. When we talk about our solar system, we're referring to the planets, moons, and other objects like asteroids and comets that orbit our sun.

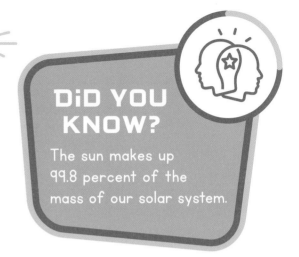

DiD YOU KNOW?

The sun makes up 99.8 percent of the mass of our solar system.

The Sun

Compared to other stars, our sun is pretty average. It's not the biggest or the smallest or the hottest or the coldest. What makes it special is that it's ours, and it's so close. With spacecraft and telescopes, we can see it in amazing detail. We can't do this with any other star.

The sun gives us light, heat, and energy. It warms our skin and makes the trees and dandelions grow. So it must be a calm, peaceful place, right?

Wrong! The sun has a temper. And when it throws temper tantrums, it flings out its insides with incredible force.

Our sun is a giant ball of electrified gas.

This gas is called **plasma**, and it's threaded with something called a **magnetic field**. Think of a

NASA/SDO

This image captured by NASA's Solar Dynamics Observatory shows active regions on the sun.

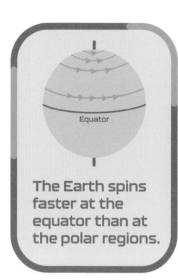

The Earth spins faster at the equator than at the polar regions.

fridge magnet. When you move a magnet away from the fridge, you feel a small tug. A magnetic field is the invisible force making that tug. And the sun is filled with these magnetic fields.

The sun spins like the Earth, but it spins faster at the equator, its midsection, than it does at its poles.

This uneven spin causes its magnetic field to twist into knots.

Try This at Home: The Rubber Band Experiment

Take a rubber band and twist it and twist it, until it starts to knot up. Then let go. It will spring out of your fingers, releasing energy. Like rubber bands, magnetic fields get so twisted up inside the sun that sometimes they explode, spewing gas out from the sun's surface.

We see these explosions from the sun as bright flashes of light called **solar flares**.

38

Relative size of Earth

Solar material explodes off the surface of the sun. The Earth is superimposed to show how small it is compared to the solar flare.

The plasma and magnetic field that a solar flare blasts out into space are called a **coronal mass ejection**. Solar flares send tremendous amounts of energy into space. In fact, a large solar flare can release as much energy as ten million volcanic eruptions.

All this activity can affect us on Earth. The radiation solar storms send out can be harmful to power grids on Earth and to astronauts in space. They also can create beautiful lights in the sky. These lights have different names, depending on where you are on Earth. They're called aurora borealis or **northern lights** near the North Pole, and aurora australis or **southern lights** near the South Pole.

Sound Smart

One average solar flare generates enough energy to power the world for one hundred thousand years.

The northern lights in Iceland

powerofforever/E+/Getty Images

We see the northern and southern lights when particles from coronal mass ejections bump into gases in Earth's magnetic field. And different gases give off different colors. When the particles from the sun bump into oxygen, you see green and yellow and red lights. Nitrogen glows blue and purple.

This beautiful light show is also a sign that Earth's magnetic field is protecting us from harmful radiation.

DiD YOU KNOW?

Auroras occur on other planets, too!
Check out these auroras on Jupiter and Saturn.

NASA/ESA/CSA/Jupiter ERS Team/ Judy Schmidt

ESA/Hubble/NASA/A. Simon (GSFC) and the OPAL Team/J. DePasquale (STScI)/L. Lamy (Observatoire de Paris)

This image of Jupiter, created from a composite of several images from the James Webb Space Telescope, shows auroras above the northern and southern poles of the planet.

This image of the auroras on Saturn's north pole region is a composite of images taken by the Hubble telescope.

Mercury

If Earth were the size of a baseball, *MERCURY* would be the size of a grape.

QUICK FACTS ABOUT MERCURY

- **DISTANCE FROM THE SUN:** 36 million miles
- **NUMBER OF MOONS:** 0
- **LENGTH OF A YEAR (ONE ORBIT OF THE SUN):** 88 Earth days
- **LENGTH OF A DAY (ONE SPIN ON ITS AXIS):** 58 Earth days

Mercury is the smallest planet in our solar system, the closest to the sun, and the fastest. It zips around the sun every 88 Earth days. Compare this to Earth, which takes 365 days to orbit the sun.

Look at a map and find a place you know that's about twenty-nine miles away from you. Now imagine traveling to that place in just one second. That's how fast Mercury travels in its orbit: twenty-nine miles a second.

You might think Mercury is superhot all over because it's so close to the sun, but it's actually a planet of extremes. On the day side, the side facing the sun, it is scorching hot; and on the night side, it is freezing cold. Daytime temperatures reach 800 degrees Fahrenheit—hot enough to melt metal—and nighttime temperatures can drop to negative 290 degrees Fahrenheit. This is because the planet has no **atmosphere** to trap heat and keep it warm at night.

An *ATMOSPHERE* is the layer of gases that surrounds a planet. On Earth, the atmosphere keeps our planet warm, protects us from harmful radiation from the sun, and contains oxygen, which supports life.

Mercury is covered in craters. And some of the craters contain ice. This ice is deep inside craters at the poles of the planet, in regions that never see sunlight.

Sound Smart

If you were somehow able to survive the extreme temperatures and stand on the surface of Mercury, our sun would appear three times larger than it does from Earth.

That's What We Know.
Here's What We Don't Know:

Scientists don't know for sure how the ice got there. One idea is that the comets that crashed into Mercury brought water and that water gathered in the coldest places on the planet.

Scientists are testing this idea, along with many others.

Venus

If Earth were the size of a baseball, **VENUS** would be the size of a tennis ball.

NASA/JPL

Venus is the hottest planet in our solar system. Scientists tried sending spacecraft to the surface, and they melted within hours of landing.

QUICK FACTS ABOUT VENUS

☐ **DISTANCE FROM THE SUN:** 67 million miles
☐ **NUMBER OF MOONS:** 0
☐ **LENGTH OF A YEAR:** 225 Earth days
☐ **LENGTH OF A DAY:** 243 Earth days

On Venus, the average temperature is a whopping *867* degrees Fahrenheit. Compare that to Earth, where the average temperature is 59 degrees.

Remember how Mercury has no atmosphere? Well, Venus is the opposite. It has too much atmosphere, and that atmosphere is 96 percent carbon dioxide, a potent greenhouse gas. This gas traps heat, baking the surface.

Venus rotates so slowly that its day is longer than its year. This means it takes longer to spin around once on its axis than it does to circle the sun. And it rotates the opposite direction of the other planets in our solar system. (Except Uranus, which also rotates backward—and on its side!)

Venus is similar to Earth in a lot of ways. It's nearly as big around as Earth and may have been formed from similar materials. Some planetary scientists believe that a long time ago, Venus had an ocean like Earth and maybe even life. But as the planet grew hotter, those oceans evaporated, filling the atmosphere with water vapor that trapped heat. In time, that water was lost to space and replaced with thick carbon dioxide from volcanoes that trapped heat even more, making Venus the fiery, hellish planet it is today.

That's What We Know.
Here's What We Don't Know:

Scientists don't know why Venus rotates in the opposite direction of the other planets. It may have been hit by a big object, like a giant asteroid, that knocked it off its rotation.

We don't know if it ever had life. We also don't know why it got so hot there. Venus is like a big red warning flag for us on Earth. Studying what happened there might give us clues for how to take care of our own planet.

Earth

QUICK FACTS ABOUT EARTH

- **DISTANCE FROM THE SUN:** 93 million miles
- **NUMBER OF MOONS:** 1
- **LENGTH OF A YEAR:** 365 days
- **LENGTH OF A DAY:** 24 hours

Earth is the biggest of the four rocky planets and the only place in our solar system we know of that has life. Earth is teeming with life. This life exists almost everywhere: in forests, deserts, mountains, lakes, wetlands, and in the ocean.

So what makes our planet so special? For one thing, Earth has a lot of liquid water. The ocean covers more than 70 percent of our planet. And life as we know it needs water to survive.

It has an atmosphere that keeps us warm and a magnetic field that protects us from the sun's harmful rays.

Earth is a planet that won't sit still. It has plates on its surface that slip and slide and knock into each other, building mountains and releasing energy as earthquakes and volcanoes.

Earth is a magical place. It gives us snowflakes and strawberries and oak trees and waterfalls. Our planet takes care of us, which is why we need to take care of it back.

About sixty years ago, astronauts visiting the moon looked back to see Earth from space and captured the photograph above.

We're used to seeing the moon rise over the Earth's surface. This, instead, was the Earth rising over the moon's surface. They called the photo *Earthrise*.

Twenty-six years later, the Voyager 1 spacecraft snapped another picture of Earth—this one from four billion miles away. Earth here is just a point of light, so tiny you can barely see it. This image became known as *The Pale Blue Dot*.

"That's here. That's home. That's us," wrote the astronomer Carl Sagan. And we have a responsibility to be kind to each other, he wrote, "and to preserve and cherish the pale blue dot, the only home we've ever known."

This image of Earth, known as *The Pale Blue Dot*, was captured from about four billion miles away by NASA's Voyager I spacecraft on February 14, 1990.

The Earth has been getting hotter in the past fifty to one hundred years. This is known as climate change.

The climate has changed many times in our planet's history, but it's different this time because humans are causing it. Most cars and buses are powered by burning fuel. Cars vent dirty exhaust from their tail pipes and power plants pump out pollution. Fossil fuels like coal and gas are burned to generate electricity. All these things release **greenhouse gases**—such as carbon dioxide, methane, and ozone—into Earth's atmosphere. Cutting down forests also releases a huge amount of greenhouse gases into the air. This is because trees are like sponges that store carbon dioxide. When they're cut down, carbon dioxide goes into the air.

The greenhouse gases act as a blanket that traps heat in the lower part of the atmosphere, keeping the planet warmer than what the sun's energy alone can provide. This is called the greenhouse effect, because the gases keep our planet warm just like glass in a greenhouse keeps plants warm. In fact, evidence from long ago suggests that when Earth loses its greenhouse effect, the planet almost entirely freezes. If the amount of greenhouse gases in the atmosphere keeps going up, the planet will continue to warm.

A hotter planet means all sorts of things. It means sea ice in Greenland, Antarctica, and the Arctic is melting, which makes our ocean waters rise. As water gets warmer, it expands, which also makes sea levels rise. Sea levels rising means more flooding along the coasts. Hotter temperatures also mean more rainfall, more powerful storms, and more wildfires, heat waves, and drought.

Our Moon

Before we had telescopes, people thought our moon was a smooth sphere. But the moon is about as smooth as a floor covered in Legos and building blocks. Its face is scarred with pits and craters, mountains and valleys, and dead volcanoes.

NASA/Goddard Space Flight Center Scientific Visualization Studio

Billions of years of getting pummeled by space rocks made the craters we see on the moon. The brighter places you see are its original crust. The darker places are hardened lava. The lava might have come from space rocks slamming into the moon and creating so much heat that they melted the moon's surface. Or these impacts might have caused magma to burst through the moon's crust.

The moon is like a giant mirror. It doesn't give off its own light. Its brightness, or "moonlight" comes from sunlight reflecting off its surface.

On the moon, there is no atmosphere, which means there's no wind or weather, nothing to wash away the marks on its surface. Because of this, the solar

DiD YOU KNOW?

The moon spends nearly as much time in the daytime sky as it does in the night sky.

system's history is preserved there. This means craters are preserved on the moon in incredible detail. So are the footprints of Neil Armstrong and other astronauts who have walked there.

Mars

If Earth were the size of a baseball, *MARS* would be the size of a Ping-Pong ball.

Mars is a cold, dusty, desert planet with iron in its soil that makes it look red. In some ways, it is more like Earth than any other planet. It has mountains, seasons, giant boulders, and polar ice caps. Wind blows the red dirt around, making dust storms. A day on Mars is only forty minutes longer than a day on Earth.

NASA/JPL-Caltech/ASU/MSSS

QUICK FACTS ABOUT MARS

- ■ **DISTANCE FROM THE SUN:** 142 million miles
- ■ **NUMBER OF MOONS:** 2
- ■ **LENGTH OF A YEAR:** 687 Earth days
- ■ **LENGTH OF A DAY:** 24.6 Earth hours

But it has a much thinner atmosphere than Earth and less gravity. It is freezing cold and bone dry.

Like Venus, scientists believe that a long time ago, Mars looked very different. They think it was once warm and wet. Water pooled into lakes and snaked through jagged rocks, carving rivers. It also had violent volcanoes.

We know a lot about Mars because we've sent lots of spacecraft there. Today, rovers like Curiosity and Perseverance drive around, poking at the dirt, digging, and collecting rocks.

Scientists say that there's evidence of ancient liquid salty water in the ground. And there's evidence that microscopic life could have once lived on Mars, or still does. But it's hard to know for sure until we can see inside the rocks and soil in labs on Earth.

But this could change soon. In an exciting—and incredibly ambitious—new mission, scientists hope to bring Martian rocks collected by the Perseverance rover back to Earth, so we can study them here. In an incredible circus act, Perseverance would load these rocks onto a rocket. The rocket would launch into orbit around Mars, and then deliver the rocks to another spacecraft, which would race them to Earth.

Jupiter

If Earth were the size of a baseball, *JUPITER* would be as big around as a semitruck tire.

Jupiter is a massive ball of hydrogen and helium gas, and the largest planet in our solar system, by far. All the other planets combined could fit inside Jupiter. So could 1,300 Earths.

NASA's Goddard Space Flight Center/Video and images courtesy of Space Telescope Science Institute

QUICK FACTS ABOUT JUPITER

- **DISTANCE FROM THE SUN:** 484 million miles
- **NUMBER OF MOONS:** 80
- **LENGTH OF A YEAR:** 12 Earth years
- **LENGTH OF A DAY:** 10 Earth hours

Jupiter is a windy, stormy planet, made up of swirling gas and liquids with an ocean of hydrogen and rings made of dust. Its famous Great Red Spot is a storm that's been raging for hundreds of years with winds that blow more than four hundred miles an

hour. On a good night, you can see the Great Red Spot through a telescope. But Jupiter has other storms that you can't see through a telescope: eight storms in its north pole and five storms in its south pole.

Jupiter has at least eighty moons that we know of. Each moon is its own world, and some of them are as interesting as the planet itself. **Europa** might have a deep saltwater ocean under a layer of ice that shoots geysers of water into space. Scientists think it's possible for life to survive below the ice. **Io** has hundreds of active volcanoes. It is oozing with hot spots and lava lakes and eruptions that blast gas hundreds of miles from its surface. **Ganymede** is the largest moon in our solar system, so big it has its own magnetic field.

Saturn

If Earth were the size of a baseball, *SATURN* would be the size of a yoga ball.

Saturn may be the most magnificent planet to look at through a telescope. This is because it has rings around it that look like a giant Hula-Hoop. These rings are made up of billions of chunks

QUICK FACTS ABOUT SATURN

- **DISTANCE FROM THE SUN:** 886 million miles
- **NUMBER OF MOONS:** 145
- **LENGTH OF A YEAR:** 29 Earth years
- **LENGTH OF A DAY:** 11 Earth hours

of ice and rock, held together by gravity. Like the sun and Jupiter, Saturn is made almost entirely of hydrogen and helium.

A spacecraft called **Cassini** took a seven-year journey to Saturn where it toured the planet for thirteen years and sent back spectacular photos. It saw Saturn's rings from every angle, along with huge storms and lightning deep within the planet.

Cassini also studied Saturn's moons, especially its largest moon, **Titan**. Titan is bigger than planet Mercury. And it's the only known world besides Earth with liquid lakes and oceans on its surface. The lakes are made of liquid methane and ethane, not water. **Enceladus**, the brightest moon in our solar system, is another ocean world that is continuously blasting geysers of icy water into space. We don't know what's lurking underneath the ice there, but, like Europa, there could very well be microscopic life.

These infrared images, taken by NASA's Cassini spacecraft, show the icy surface of Saturn's moon Titan.

NASA/JPL-Caltech/University of Nantes/University of Arizona

Uranus

If Earth were the size of a baseball, *URANUS* would be the size of a standard globe.

QUICK FACTS ABOUT URANUS

- **DISTANCE FROM THE SUN:** 1.8 billion miles
- **NUMBER OF MOONS:** 27
- **LENGTH OF A YEAR:** 84 Earth years
- **LENGTH OF A DAY:** 17 Earth hours

Only one spacecraft has ever flown close enough to Uranus and Neptune to see them, so we know less about these two planets. We know that they're ice giants, similar to each other in many ways, except Uranus lies on its side as it orbits.

Methane in Uranus's atmosphere makes it look bluish green. It has thirteen faint rings that are made from ice and dust.

Uranus is not the farthest planet from our sun, but it's the coldest.

The smallest of its moons, **Miranda**, has some really weird features. Ancient craters and valleys and ridges and deep, deep canyons all look like bulges, wrinkles, and weird patches on its surface.

Neptune

If Earth were the size of a baseball, *NEPTUNE* would be the size of a frying pan.

QUICK FACTS ABOUT NEPTUNE

- **DISTANCE FROM THE SUN:** 2.8 billion miles
- **NUMBER OF MOONS:** 14
- **LENGTH OF A YEAR:** 165 Earth years
- **LENGTH OF A DAY:** 16 Earth hours

Neptune, a cold, icy world, is the farthest known planet in our solar system. It is also the windiest. Winds whip around the planet faster than the speed of sound.

Neptune is so far from the sun that it takes nearly 165 Earth years to make a complete orbit. In fact, since it was discovered in 1846, it has only made one orbit around the sun.

Because of its distance from the sun, the brightest part of its day would look like the dimmest twilight on Earth.

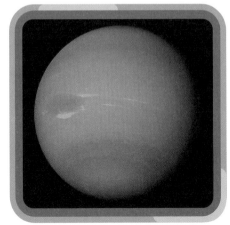

NASA/Voyager/JPL Caltech

NASA's Voyager 2 spacecraft is the only one to have ever seen Neptune up close. At the time, it photographed a Great Dark Spot on the planet, but later images by the Hubble Space Telescope showed that spot had vanished.

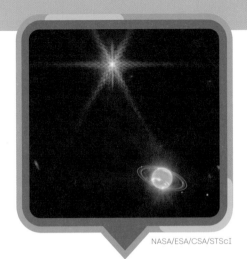

NASA/ESA/CSA/STScI

This image of Neptune from the James Webb Space Telescope shows its rings.

That's What We Know.
Here's What We Don't Know:

Why are the winds on Neptune so fast? What happened to its Great Dark Spot? Scientists don't know what the spot was or what happened to it.

And then there are the dwarf planets. There's **Pluto**, the biggest of the little planets. In fact, for a long time, it was considered a regular planet. Pluto is located so far away that it took nine and a half years for a spacecraft to journey there. But the pictures it took were spectacular, showing towering mountains and canyons as deep as the Grand Canyon. It is believed to be covered in mostly nitrogen ice, which is gooey like toothpaste. And a giant heart-shaped region stretches across its surface.

This enhanced-color image of Pluto was taken by the New Horizons spacecraft on July 14, 2015.

NASA/Johns Hopkins University Applied Physics Laboratory/Southwest Research Institute

Haumea is shaped like a football. Ceres has mysterious bright spots. Makemake and Eris are icy, rocky worlds, which, like Haumea, orbit in a faraway region called the Kuiper Belt.

And that's not all. In addition to all the planets and moons, our solar system is chock-full of flying space rocks and ice balls. Asteroids, comets, and meteoroids race around, crashing into moons and planets, carving craters, melting rocks, and sometimes leaving ice where they land.

CHAPTER FOUR

HUMANS IN SPACE

Look up at the sky. Now imagine traveling 250 miles up, through clouds, through the Earth's upper atmosphere and then farther up into space—that's about the distance between Washington, DC, and New York City. There, a satellite that orbits the Earth is a home for astronauts. For many months at a time, astronauts live and work and eat and sleep and play there.

The **International Space Station** is the size of a football field.

NASA Johnson/Flickr

Jessica Watkins, a NASA astronaut, looks out at Earth from inside the cupola in the International Space Station.

The International Space Station

Inside, there are eight bedrooms, four bathrooms, a gym, lots of laboratory space, and a big bay window where astronauts can stare down at Earth.

Inside the International Space Station, astronauts float from room to room. They do scientific research, harvest vegetables, take care of the station, and study how the human body responds to life in space.

A view of the southwest coast of Australia from the International Space Station

NASA astronaut **Victor Glover** working inside Japan's Kibo laboratory on the International Space Station. He is installing gear that will help the astronauts research how spaceflight affects the human body.

NASA Johnson/Flickr

They put on space suits, open the hatch, and go out into outer space itself to check or repair equipment. These are called space walks.

An astronaut (**Matthias Maurer** of the European Space Agency) works to install gear on the outside of the International Space Station during a space walk.

NASA Johnson/Flickr

Living in Space

Living in space has challenges you never think about on Earth.

On the International Space Station, everything is weightless. Astronauts float, and so does everything else onboard—screwdrivers, scissors, and toilet paper, for example. So everything has to be Velcroed or tied down. And when things get away from you, they can be hard to find.

In microgravity, there's no up or down, no difference between floor and ceiling. That means astronauts bounce from wall to ceiling like Spider-Man. They push off with their feet and use their hands to move around, pulling themselves from handrail to handrail.

Sound Smart

Have you ever been on a roller coaster with a big drop? You might have noticed that it feels a little like you're floating up as you're falling. That's what's happening on the International Space Station—all the time. The station is in constant freefall around the Earth as it orbits, and in freefall, everything falls at the same rate. This state is known as **microgravity.**

NASA astronaut Megan McArthur has done two tours in space and recently spent 199 days living on the International Space Station. She called living in microgravity "just a tremendous amount of fun. I wish everyone could get to experience it." She said, "Essentially you feel like you're flying."

"What I quickly learned to do was I'd find a handrail on any available surface, and I would tuck my feet in and perch halfway up the wall or on the ceiling. I found it's an interesting way to view everything that was going on around you and just enjoy that space."
—NASA astronaut Megan McArthur

Eating in Space

Imagine sucking pureed beef out of a toothpaste tube. Gross, right? That was space food for the earliest astronauts.

The food that astronauts eat can't take up much space, and it has to stay good for many months without spoiling. Astronauts also can't eat anything that might leave crumbs, because crumbs could float around and clog sensitive equipment. The solution is food that's freeze-dried: That means all water has been sucked out of it.

NASA Johnson/Flickr

Food has gotten better since the early space days. On the station, astronauts now add

NASA astronaut and Expedition 67 Flight Engineer **Kjell N. Lindgren** prepares to eat a taco aboard the International Space Station.

NASA astronaut Megan McArthur with fresh peppers and avocados onboard the International Space Station.

water back to their food and heat it in an oven to make it more food-like. And they have hundreds of choices now. They eat pulled beef brisket, macaroni and cheese, and mango fruit salad—even chocolate cake.

They chomp bites of food from the air as it floats in front of them. Oh, and sometimes they eat upside down from their fellow astronauts.

Instead of using plates, which would float away, they often wrap food in tortillas.

NASA Johnson/Flickr

Fresh apples and oranges float weightless between crew members in microgravity on the International Space Station.

Fresh oranges and grapefruits are sometimes delivered during a resupply mission as a special treat.

WEIRD THINGS THAT SPACE DOES TO THE BODY:

- In microgravity, the spine expands, and astronauts get as much as 3 percent taller.

- Body fluids shift up toward the head, so during the first few days in space, astronauts' faces get puffy looking, and they have to pee a lot.

- This puts pressure on the eyes too and can make things blurry.

- Since muscles and bones aren't needed to support the body in microgravity, they shrink without lots of exercise.

Exercising in Space

Exercise is especially important in space. This is because bones and muscles lose strength when they're not holding the weight of the body. To prevent bone and muscle loss, astronauts exercise two and a half hours each day. They have treadmills, exercise bikes, and machines for weight training. And they have to be strapped into their equipment with harnesses, clips, and bungee cords.

Fun

Days are long on the International Space Station, and astronauts work hard. But they have fun, too. Onboard the space station, they read books, watch movies, and take dazzling pictures of Earth out the window.

DiD YOU KNOW?

In 2013, Canadian astronaut Chris Hadfield performed David Bowie's song "Space Oddity" on an acoustic guitar from the International Space Station. Bowie himself called it "possibly the most poignant version of the song ever created."

The **cupola of the International Space Station** is a great place for astronaut Megan McArthur to read a book and see the Atlantic Ocean below.

They twist and turn and flip like acrobats. They do the "long jump," which means pushing off from one end of the space station with their feet to see how far they can fly. They play soccer and card games and read books and watch the Super Bowl from space.

Sleeping in Space

On the space station, there's no difference between night and day. In fact, every twenty-four hours, astronauts see the sun rise and set sixteen times as they circle the Earth. To keep their bodies on a sleep schedule, they set the lights to the brightest setting during the workday, dim the lights when the workday is over, so it feels like evening, and then turn them off when it's time to sleep.

Astronauts sleep in sleeping bags that are tied to a wall in tiny closet-like rooms called **crew quarters**. Their arms go through sleeping bag holes, and the bag zips up like a jacket. Without gravity, you don't need a pillow. As you relax and fall asleep, your arms float up and your head tips forward, zombielike.

DiD YOU KNOW?

Astronauts on the space station see a sunrise every ninety minutes—that's less than the time it takes to watch the movie *Encanto*.

Going to the Bathroom in Space

If you ask Megan McArthur how you go to the bathroom in space, she'll tell you "Very, very carefully." Because *everything* floats. So astronauts pee into a funnel and poop into a tiny hole that sucks away the waste. And then most of that pee gets turned into drinking water. A machine on the station uses powerful filters to turn the urine and sweat into water that's safe to drink. It might sound like the grossest kind of recycling, but when treated, it's just as pure as any water we drink on Earth. And astronauts swear that it tastes great.

Recycling Water in Space

One of Megan McArthur's jobs during her space station mission was to experiment with the technology that recycles water. Right now, 85 percent of the water on the space station gets recycled. The hope is to get that number up to above 95 percent. This will be helpful to astronauts traveling to the moon or Mars and also on Earth in areas without access to clean water.

Early Space Travel

Astronauts have been traveling to space for more than sixty years. The first human in space was Russian cosmonaut Yuri Gagarin. On April 12, 1961, he circled the Earth once in a space capsule, which then fell back toward Earth. Gagarin ejected from the capsule about four miles from the ground and parachuted to landing while his capsule fell separately to the ground in Kazakhstan.

Sound Smart

Astronaut comes from the Greek words meaning "space sailor."

A month later, Alan Shepard became the first American in space. These milestones achieved by the Soviet Union and the United States were part of what's known as the **space race**, a period after World War II in which the United States and Russia competed to dominate in space. Each country scrambled to prove itself superior.

In the next four years, Russia achieved the record for the longest solo spaceflight and the first space walk.

Then the United States beat out Russia for the most time spent in space—two weeks.

But what the US president at the time, John F. Kennedy, *really* wanted was to send people to the moon.

That happened in July 1969. Three astronauts blasted into space on the Apollo 11 spacecraft, and then two of the astronauts flew a smaller "lunar lander" named Eagle to the moon's surface. Just before 10:00 p.m. Houston time, with 650 million people watching from their television sets, Neil Armstrong became the first person ever to walk on the moon. "That's one small step for man, one giant leap for mankind," he famously said as he took his first step.

On the Moon

Neil Armstrong and Buzz Aldrin, who flew on that first moon mission, are among only twelve people who have ever set foot on the moon. It's been fifty years since anyone's been there.

NASA

But we know a lot from the time they spent there. Those twelve astronauts planted flags, hit golf balls, and left a plaque that said: "We came in peace for all mankind." Walking on the moon feels like walking on a trampoline, and it smells like burnt gunpowder, or ashes in a fireplace, astronauts have said. From the moon, the sky is black and the sun is bright. Meanwhile, Earth looks like a blue marble hanging in space.

On July 20, 1969, Buzz Aldrin walked on the surface of the moon. Mission commander Neil Armstrong took the photo.

DiD YOU KNOW?

On the moon, gravity is six times as weak as it is on Earth, so you can jump six times as high. That means, from a standing position, you could easily jump a foot higher than the height of the tallest basketball player.

What's Next?

NASA, America's space agency, is planning to send people back to the moon. For a future mission called Artemis III, a crew of astronauts will land near the moon's south pole and then take a journey around its surface. NASA's longer-term plans are more ambitious. The hope is to build another space station, this time in orbit around the moon, and a "base camp" on the surface of the moon where people can work and sleep for weeks at a time.

This mission to the moon will also help NASA prepare for the next big exploration: sending humans to Mars. Living on Mars won't be easy. For one thing, because Mars is thirty-four million miles away at its closest orbit, it could take about 250 days to travel there. That's nearly an entire school year. That means help would be far away and a Martian astronaut would have to be resourceful to survive.

They'll need to live in a dome, grow plants in greenhouses, and extract water from Martian ice.

To go outside, they'll need to wear protective suits that pump oxygen. This is because carbon dioxide, which is poisonous to humans at high concentrations, makes up most of the Martian air, which contains hardly any oxygen. Also, the atmospheric pressure is so low that without protection, your blood would boil.

Sound Smart

Only one-tenth of 1 percent of the air on Mars is made up of oxygen. That's not even close to enough oxygen to survive.

Still, imagine being the first person ever to live on another planet—the ultimate adventure.

Would you do it?

CHAPTER FIVE

THE UNKNOWN

For the longest time, scientists thought planets circling other stars would look just like our solar system. They figured they'd have neat, circular orbits. They thought they'd find small rocky planets close to the sun and giant gas and ice planets farther out.

Instead, they found a planet orbiting another live star, an **exoplanet**, and it wasn't at all what they'd expected: It was bigger than Saturn and orbiting closer to its sun than Earth. This planet, in a star system called 51 Pegasi, would become known as a "hot Jupiter."

Planet formation is messy and chaotic. And we now know that many solar systems don't look anything like ours. 51 Pegasi was found in 1995. Since then, astronomers have found more than five thousand planets orbiting other stars. They come in all different shapes and sizes.

There are hot Jupiters and super Earths and puff planets and lava monsters. There are planets that orbit dead stars, called

This exoplanet, Kepler-1649c, is similar to Earth in size and temperature and exists in its star's habitable zone where liquid water could exist. This image shows an artist's imagining of the red dwarf star rising over the Kepler horizon.

pulsars. There are egg-shaped planets, planets with wacky orbits, and planets that orbit two or even more stars at once. Imagine living on a planet with three suns in the sky!

We now know that our universe is crowded with exoplanets. In fact, most stars have planets orbiting them. So if you want to see a star with an exoplanet, go outside and point at a star, and chances are you are also pointing to a planet orbiting that star. There are many, many exoplanets still waiting to be found.

Most of the planets we know about have been found with powerful telescopes like Kepler, **TESS**, and **CoRoT**. On Christmas Day in 2021, a new telescope launched: the **James Webb Space Telescope**, the biggest, most powerful space telescope ever built. This new telescope is changing planet hunting as we know it.

The Webb telescope can study the atmosphere of an exoplanet, which can tell us a lot about that planet's story. For example, it

The James Webb Space Telescope as imagined by an artist.

NASA GSFC/CIL/Adriana Manrique Gutierrez/NASA's James Webb Space Telescope/Flickr

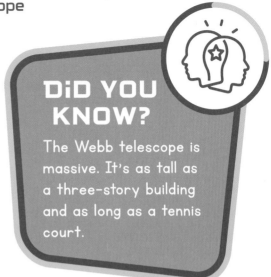

DID YOU KNOW?

The Webb telescope is massive. It's as tall as a three-story building and as long as a tennis court.

might find high levels of sulfur dioxide, which would mean an environment that's toxic to humans. Or it might find some of the same molecules found on Earth, like oxygen or carbon dioxide. These could be ingredients for life.

Are We Alone in the Universe?

It may be the most pressing question in astronomy. Is there life beyond Earth? And perhaps even more interesting, is there intelligent life beyond Earth? We don't know the answer yet. But scientists are looking hard. Really hard.

Evidence for life could take many forms. Rocky exoplanets with atmospheric chemistry like ours. Signs of water on Mars. Lights from technology shining out from other worlds.

Most exoplanets are too far away for us to ever travel to them. But being able to measure what makes up the atmospheres of other planets with Webb is a game changer.

Scientists think the atmospheres of planets with life will look dramatically different than those without life. Oxygen and methane are gases produced by living things. So if we find a planet with a lot of oxygen and methane, that might mean there are things growing and breathing there. Likewise, Earth's atmosphere might be a giveaway to an alien on another planet that there's life here.

A **biosignature** is something that can be used as evidence for life. Oxygen and methane in an exoplanet's atmosphere would be a biosignature.

A **technosignature** is evidence of technology on another planet.

Sound Smart

When single-celled algae evolved on Earth, they started making oxygen, and the composition of the Earth's atmosphere changed forever.

What Is That Flying Thing?

In September 2017, an astronomer spotted something strange through a telescope: an object tumbling at extraordinarily high speeds through our solar system, not bound by gravity to our sun. It was so far away we couldn't see much, and it zoomed by fast. It was either shaped like a hot dog or a pancake. And it was like nothing astronomers had ever seen.

It was given the name **'Oumuamua** (say: oh MOO-uh MOO-uh), which means "scout" or "messenger."

There were lots of ideas and arguments over what the thing

was. Maybe, just maybe, it was an alien spaceship, some said. But nearly all astronomers agree that it was a rock from another planetary system. For example, a chunk of a Pluto-like planet in another star system that was knocked off by an asteroid and sent flying. Or a cosmic iceberg.

It's not the only mystery. What used to be called UFOs, or unidentified flying objects, now have a new name in science: **unidentified anomalous phenomena**, or UAPs. And between 2004 and 2021, the government reported 144 of these on our planet, only one of which could be explained. Some share similar characteristics. On more than one occasion, pilots described seeing something that looked like a giant white Tic Tac.

An artist imagines 'Oumuamua passing through our solar system.

European Southern Observatory/M. Kornmesser/ NASA Goddard Space Flight Center/Flickr

Do Aliens Exist?

Detecting alien signals isn't easy. We keep thinking we've found a radio signal from another world only to discover it's just a stray signal from Earth. But the probability that there is intelligent life is high. Some scientists who devote their life to this say it's a question of *when* we'll find life, not *if* we'll find it.

But extraordinary claims need extraordinary evidence.

Scientists need a lot of evidence to be convinced. And it will be a long journey to get enough evidence to say that yes, there is life beyond Earth.

Scientists have been searching for radio signals from other planets for more than one hundred years. To find them, they use giant radio telescopes, like a telescope in China called FAST. FAST is 1,640 feet, or about six city blocks across. It's big enough to hold twenty billion bowls of cornflakes. It's like having a humongous eye on the sky.

Final Thoughts

Maybe someday we'll find that the universe is full of intelligent life. Maybe other planets have science and music and art and poetry. Maybe they have roller coasters and fidget spinners and foosball. Maybe we can learn from them how to live together in peace, and how to take better care of our planet.

And if we never find evidence of life, that would be profound, too. It would mean Earth is even more special than we realize.

Hundreds of years ago, the solar eclipse was the great mystery, dazzling and magical and utterly peculiar. Now that our technology is more advanced, we've solved that mystery, but are stumped by so many more:

- How did Venus get so hot?
- Is there life on Mars?
- Did anything exist before the big bang?
- Is there intelligent life beyond our solar system?
- How do we best protect our planet?

And what we need, what we really need, is for young people to grow up to become space explorers and scientists who solve these mysteries for us.

Maybe that's you.

WHAT DO YOU REMEMBER?

On the following pages there are some tough questions to put your knowledge to the test! Use this book as a resource for help.

Introduction and Chapter One

1. What are some examples of how animals act before and during a total solar eclipse?

2. What is it that we can see *only* during a total solar eclipse?

3. What is a star?

4. Make a list of things you can see in the night sky with just your eyes (no telescope or binoculars).

5. Plan your own stargazing tool kit. What will you put in it?

6. What are two reasons one star might look brighter than another star?

7. If it takes four years for light to travel from Proxima Centauri to our sun, how many light-years apart are the two stars?

8. Why is looking at stars kind of like time traveling?

9. How many constellations have you seen?

10. Explain how to find Polaris in the night sky for your parents or friends.

Chapter Two

1. Describe the big bang.

2. When did the big bang occur?

3. It's unknown whether there was anything before the big bang. What do you think?

4. Draw and label a helium atom and a hydrogen atom.

5. What are a couple of examples of things that gravity does in space? What does it do on Earth?

6. What did astronomer Carl Sagan mean when he said, "We are made of star stuff"?

7. What are two ways that stars die?

8. What is happening to the distance between galaxies in our universe?

9. What is it that's keeping planets and humans and solar systems from stretching as the universe expands?

Chapter Three

1. What is wrong with most of the pictures we see of our solar system?

2. What causes energy to burst from the sun as solar flares?

3. How can solar storms affect us on Earth?

4. Why is planet Mercury so hot during the day and so cold at night?

5. What does it mean that a day on Venus is longer than a year?

6. What makes our planet Earth so special?

7. Why do footprints, ancient craters, and other markings stay preserved on the moon?

8. How is Mars similar to Earth? How is it different?

9. What is the Great Red Spot on Jupiter?

10. Why do you think it's important to study and learn more about outer space?

Chapter Four

1. Describe the International Space Station. Would you want to live there? Why or why not?

2. What kind of work do astronauts do on the International Space Station?

3. What is microgravity? Why do people float on the International Space Station?

4. Why is most of the food astronauts eat in space freeze-dried?

5. Describe three things that living in space does to the human body.

6. Why is it so important that astronauts exercise a *lot* in space?

7. What would you do for fun if you were an astronaut on the International Space Station?

8. How many people have walked on the moon, and how long has it been since anyone has been there?

9. Describe some of the challenges of living on Mars. Would you do it?

10. If you had to describe today's space race, what do you think it would be?

Chapter Five

1. What is an exoplanet?

2. Why was "51 Pegasi b," the first exoplanet discovered around a live star, so surprising to scientists?

3. How common are exoplanets?

4. What might evidence for life beyond Earth look like?

5. What is an example of a biosignature? What's an example of a technosignature?

6. How might aliens from far away be able to figure out that Earth has life?

7. Do you think there's life beyond Earth? Do you think there's intelligent life beyond Earth? Draw a picture of what intelligent life might look like.

8. Why would finding out that there's no intelligent life beyond Earth be a powerful discovery, too?

9. If you could devote your life to solving one big scientific problem about Earth or space, what would it be?

GLOSSARY

Alpha Centauri: The closest star system to our sun. It is made up of three stars: Alpha Centauri A, Alpha Centauri B, and Proxima Centauri, the closest star to our sun.

Asteroid: A small, rocky object that orbits the sun like a planet. Most can be found in the asteroid belt between Mars and Jupiter.

Astronomical unit: The average distance between the Earth and the sun, ninety-three million miles. It is the unit of measurement used to determine the distance between objects in our solar system.

Astronomy: The study of everything outside Earth's atmosphere, including stars, planets, and space.

Atmosphere: The layer of gases that surrounds a planet.

Atoms: The basic building blocks of matter. Each atom is made up of protons, neutrons, and electrons.

Big bang: The idea that the universe began as a single, infinitely hot, dense point that suddenly began to grow, fast, in every direction, and then expanded and stretched over 13.8 billion years to become the size it is now. And it's still expanding.

Biosignature: Something that can be used as evidence of life.

Black hole: The result of a massive star collapsing, an extremely dense object with a gravitational pull so strong that nothing, not even light, can escape it.

Cassini: A spacecraft that toured Saturn for thirteen years, studying the planet and its moons, and sent back spectacular photos.

Comets: Objects made of dust and frozen gases that orbit the sun.

Constellation: A group of stars that forms a picture or shape.

Corona: The sun's outer atmosphere. It can be seen during a total solar eclipse.

Coronal mass ejection: The plasma and magnetic field that a solar flare blasts out into space.

CoRoT: CoRoT, short for Convection, Rotation and planetary Transits, is a planet-hunting space telescope launched by the European Space Agency and the French Space Agency.

Crew quarters: The tiny rooms on the International Space Station where astronauts sleep.

Earth: The biggest of the four rocky planets and the only planet we know of that has life.

Ecliptic: The imaginary line that shows the sun's path across our sky. The planets and the moon move along a similar track.

Enceladus: A Saturn moon, Enceladus is the brightest moon in our solar system and blasts plumes of icy water from an underground ocean into space.

Europa: A moon of Jupiter. Scientists have evidence that beneath its icy surface, Europa has a saltwater ocean.

Exoplanet: A planet that orbits a star other than our sun.

Galaxy: A collection of billions of stars and their solar systems, all held together by gravity. Our galaxy is called the Milky Way.

Ganymede: One of Jupiter's moons. Ganymede is the largest moon in our solar system, so big it has its own magnetic field.

Gravity: The force that keeps us grounded, keeps all planets in orbit around the sun, and keeps moons in orbit around planets.

Greenhouse gases: Gases that trap heat in the Earth's atmosphere, making the planet hotter over time.

International Space Station: A large spacecraft and science laboratory that orbits the Earth and is a home to astronauts.

Io: One of Jupiter's moons and the most volcanically active body in our solar system.

James Webb Space Telescope: The biggest, most powerful space telescope ever built, Webb launched on Christmas Day in 2021.

Jupiter: A gas giant and the largest planet in our solar system.

Light pollution: City lights and other bright lights making the night sky brighter. This can make it difficult to see stars and planets in the sky. Light pollution also interferes with bird migration.

Light-year: The distance that light travels in one year. This unit is used to measure vast distances in space.

Luminosity: A measure of the brightness of a star, or how much energy the star puts out.

Magnetic field: A field of force created inside a star or planet.

Mars: The fourth planet from the sun. Mars has iron in its soil that makes it look red.

Mercury: Mercury is the smallest and the fastest planet in our solar system and the one closest to the sun.

Meteor shower: Dust and debris seen when Earth crosses a comet's orbit.

Microgravity: A condition in which gravity is so small that people and things appear weightless and float.

Milky Way: The spiral, or Frisbee-shaped galaxy that includes our solar system.

Miranda: The smallest of the Uranus moons, Miranda is full of strange features, like ridges, valleys, and deep, deep canyons that look like bulges and wrinkles on its surface.

Nebula: A massive cloud of gas and dust in space. In some nebulas, new stars are being formed. Others come from gas and dust thrown out by dying stars.

Neptune: The farthest known planet in our solar system, it is also the windiest.

Neutron star: The hot, extremely dense core of a star that was too large to become a white dwarf but too small to become a black hole.

Northern and southern lights: A spectacular display of lights near the Earth's poles, these are caused when charged particles collide with gases in Earth's upper magnetic field. They are also called aurora borealis near the North Pole and aurora australis near the South Pole.

Orbit: The path an object takes as it goes around another object.

'Oumuamua: A mysterious object spotted through a telescope in 2017 that scientists believe came from another planetary system.

Planetary nebula: A region of gas and dust shed from the outer layers of a dying star.

Plasma: A highly energized form of gas. The sun is made of plasma.

Pluto: A dwarf planet beyond Neptune's orbit, Pluto was considered for a long time to be the ninth planet in our solar system.

Proxima Centauri: The closest star to our sun.

Red dwarf: The smallest and coolest type of star and the most common type of star in the universe.

Red giant: A star that has consumed all the hydrogen at its core and started the process of dying. The core uses helium as fuel, the shell surrounding the core starts fusing hydrogen itself, and the star expands to a giant size. Most stars become red giants before collapsing as white dwarfs or exploding as supernovas.

Red-light flashlight: A flashlight with a red lens that helps you see things while stargazing without losing your night vision.

Satellite: This usually refers to a machine that orbits a moon, planet, or star. But the moon and Earth are satellites, too, orbiting Earth and the sun, respectively.

Saturn: The second largest planet in our solar system, Saturn is known for its icy rings.

Shooting star: A glowing streak of light that's seen when meteors, or chunks of comets and asteroids, enter Earth's atmosphere.

Sirius: Also known as the Dog Star or Sirius A, Sirius is the brightest star in the night sky.

Solar: Anything related to the sun.

Solar flare: A sudden explosion of energy from the surface of the sun.

Solar system: The solar system is what we call our planetary system because the word *solar* is related to our host star, the sun. Our solar system includes everything bound by gravity that orbits our sun, including eight planets, dwarf planets, moons, and other objects like asteroids and comets.

Space race: The period after World War II when the United States and Russia competed to dominate in space.

Star: A glowing ball of hot gas, held together by its own gravity. Hydrogen atoms inside the core fuse, forming helium and creating pressure, which pushes the star out as the gravity pushes it in. Nuclear fusion makes the star shine.

Stellar nebula: A cloud of gas and dust where stars are born.

Sun: Our host star and a giant ball of electrified gas.

Supernova: The largest supergiant stars explode powerfully into supernovas at the end of their lives, violently flinging their outer layers to space in explosions that can briefly outshine entire galaxies.

Technosignature: Evidence of technology on another planet.

TESS: NASA's Transiting Exoplanet Survey Satellite, or TESS, scans and maps sectors of the sky and discovers exoplanets.

Titan: Saturn's largest moon. It has lakes of methane and ethane on its surface.

Total solar eclipse: When the moon passes between the Earth and the sun, totally blocking out the sun's light.

Unidentified anomalous phenomena: Unidentified objects in our sky. These were formerly called UFOs, or unidentified flying objects.

Uranus: The third largest planet in our solar system, an icy giant like Neptune, Uranus lies on its side as it orbits.

Venus: The hottest planet in our solar system and the second from the sun.

White dwarf: The slowly cooling core of a small or medium mass star that has recently died. Many billions of years from now, our sun will shed its outer layers to space, leaving behind the white dwarf core at its center.

Yellow dwarf: A kind of star that includes our sun.

ACKNOWLEDGMENTS

I am indebted to the following scientists and experts who gave their time in interviews and fact-checking:

ELISABETH ADAMS, senior scientist, Planetary Science Institute

GIADA ARNEY, research space scientist, Planetary Studies, NASA's Goddard Space Flight Center

DEBORAH DOMINGUE, senior scientist, Planetary Science Institute

ALEX FILIPPENKO, Distinguished Professor of Astronomy, University of California, Berkeley

KEITH HAWKINS, Associate Professor, Department of Astronomy, University of Texas at Austin

DAVID JACKSON, Associate Professor, Department of Mathematics, Science, and Social Studies Education, University of Georgia

MEGAN MCARTHUR, oceanographer, engineer, and NASA astronaut

JON MEYER, meteorologist and climate scientist, Utah Climate Center, Utah State University

JESSICA NOVIELLO, planetary geologist, NASA Postdoctoral Management Program, fellow at NASA Goddard Space Flight Center

LYNNAE C. QUICK, associate branch head, Planetary Geology, Geophysics and Geochemistry Laboratory and ocean worlds planetary scientist, NASA Goddard Space Flight Center

MICHELLE THALLER, astronomer and science communicator, NASA

DAN WERTHIMER, chief scientist, Berkeley SETI Research Center, University of California, Berkeley

C. ALEX YOUNG, Associate Director for Science, Heliophysics Science Division, NASA's Goddard Space Flight Center

Thank you to Nicholas Magliato for his editorial guidance and sharp editing eye, and for having an answer to every question. I can't imagine working with a more supportive editor. To the team at Penguin Random House who made this better every step of the way. A million thank-yous to the copy editors, fact-checkers, and designers. To my early readers, for their help and insight: Heather DeCaluwe, Vanessa Dennis, Parker Fadoul, Elizabeth Landau, Carl Lydick, Ellie Redmond, Charles Russell, Wendy Thomas Russell, and Lonnie Shekhtman. To Brooke Brown, for helping me see into the life of things during our walks. To Parker, for the support and space to write this. To my parents, for always modeling a love of reading and learning.

And above all, to Autumn and Kai, the two brightest stars in my sky, for all your weird and wonderful questions that made me want to write this book.